a gift for

_____

from

_____

BABIES

with love

M·I·L·K

MOMENTS INTIMACY LAUGHTER KINSHIP

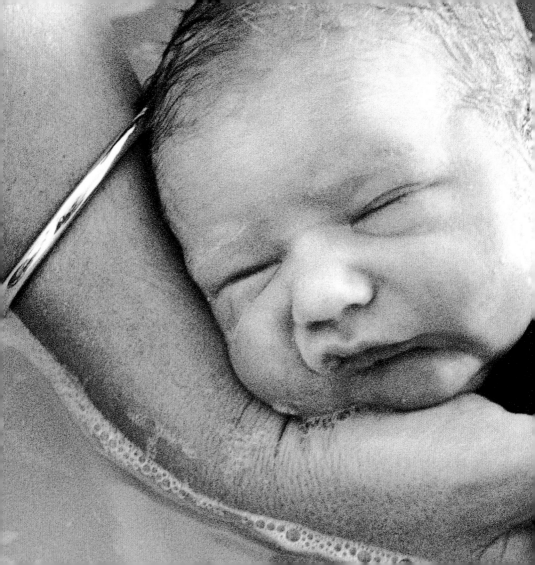

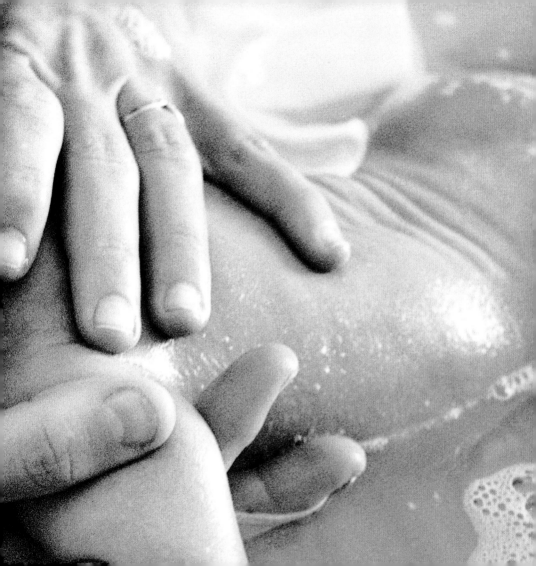

Innocence is the child,

and forgetfulness,

a new beginning,

a game, a self-rolling wheel, a first movement,

a Holy Yea.

[FRIEDRICH NIETZSCHE]

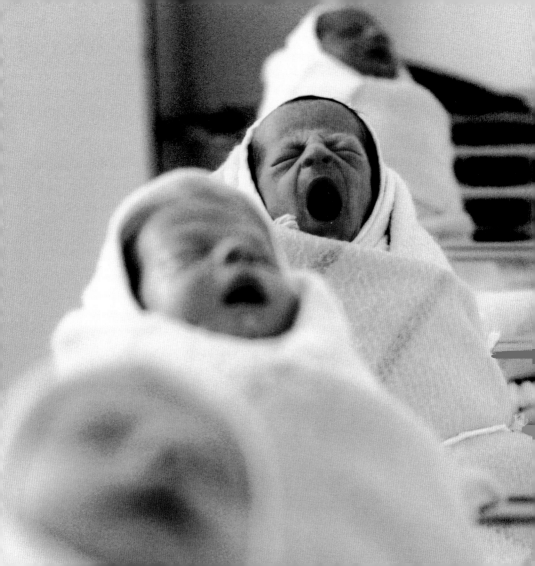

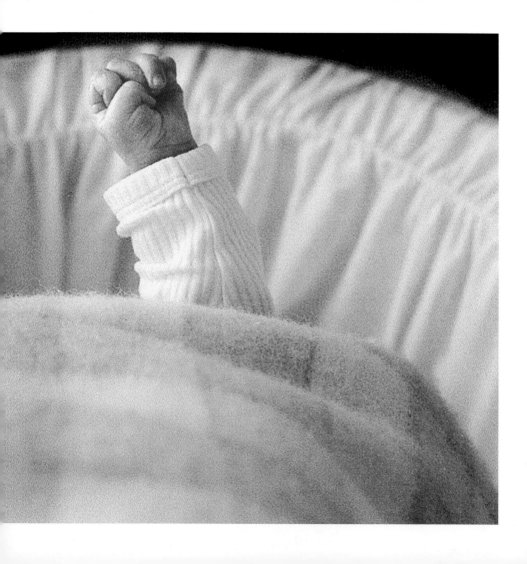

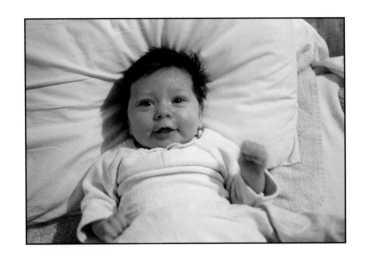

Every newborn baby is a newborn hope.

[PAM BROWN]

Before you were conceived I wanted you.
Before you were born I loved you.
Before you were here an hour I would die for you.
This is the miracle of life.

[MAUREEN HAWKINS]

So small – the fulcrum
of our lives,
the pivot of our universe.

[PAM BROWN]

Your priorities change, everything changes,

but the biggest change

is that you love somebody in a way that you never loved before.

[DIANE KEATON]

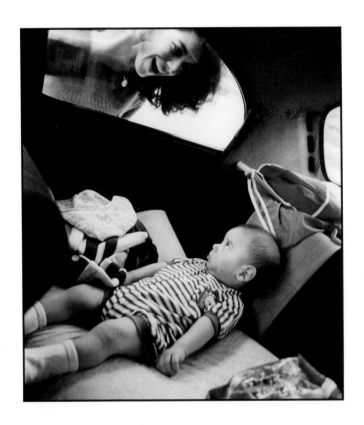

For this **small life** you would gladly give your own.

No one told you it would be like this. No one ever can.

[PAM BROWN]

A baby costs more
than anything else on earth.
Your love,
your life.

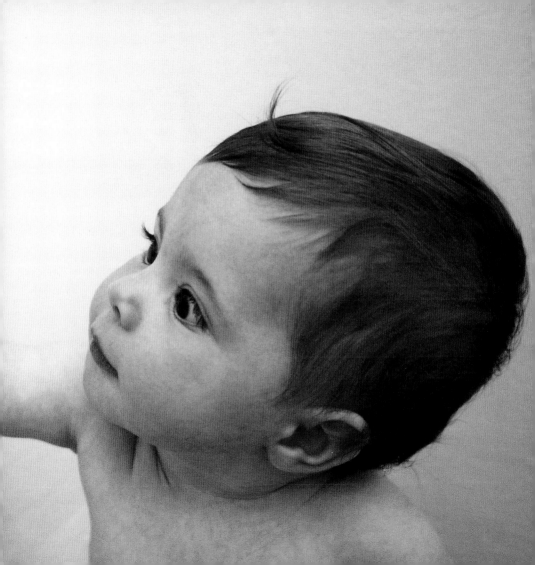

I do not love him because he is good,
but because he is my little child.

{RABINDRANATH TAGORE}

No man can possibly know what life means,

what the world means,

what anything means, until he has a child and loves it.

And then the whole universe changes

and nothing will ever again seem exactly as it seemed before.

[LAFCADIO HEARN]

When we hear the baby laugh,
it is the **loveliest thing** that can happen to us.

[SIGMUND FREUD]

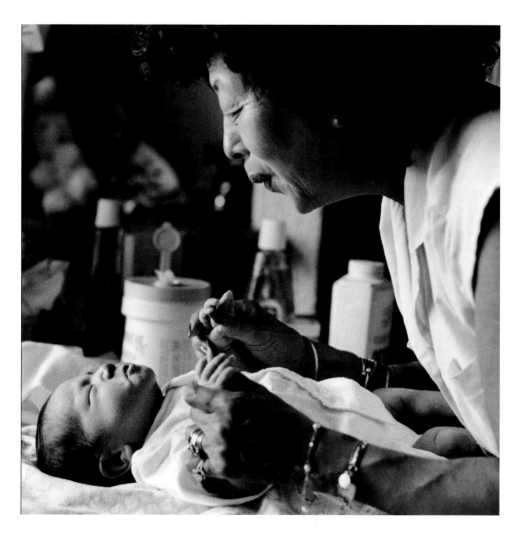

Babies are smaller, louder, more unpredictable than parents had expected.
But far more wonderful. Far more precious.

[PAM BROWN]

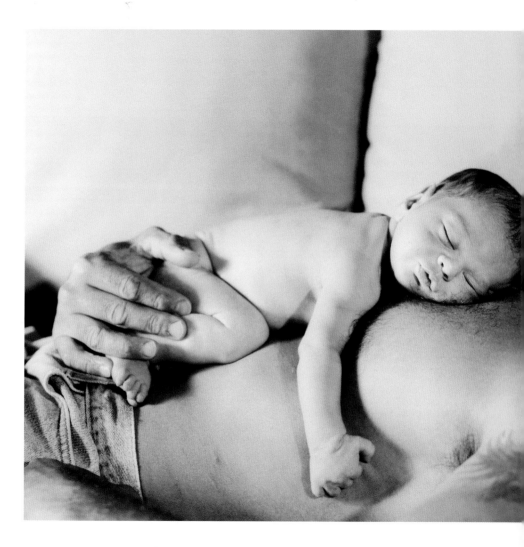

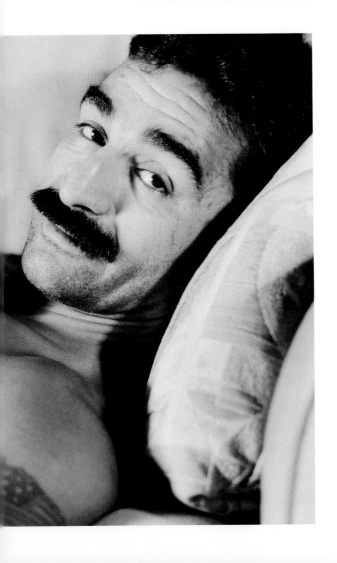

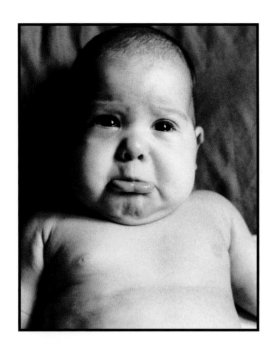

A baby's thumb is minuscule – but you are firmly under it.

[CHARLOTTE GRAY]

We find a delight in the
beauty and happiness
of children that makes the heart
too big for the body.

[RALPH WALDO EMERSON]

...This picture of me, and my Thomas,
my angel – it's a picture of love.

[KIM PHUC]

Shared laughter. Bath times and play times. Sudden smiles.

New marvels every day – first word, first step, first everything.

A life less simple

– but richer than you could have ever dreamed.

[PAM BROWN]

Family faces are magic mirrors.

All babies bring Spring back to the world.

[PAM BROWN]

Page 2
© Venkata Sunder Rao
Pampana (Sunder), India
A tender touch – a young girl looks after her baby sister asleep in a hammock made from her mother's sari. Without a permanent home, the family lives on the streets of Vijayawada in India.

Pages 4–5
© **Kelvin Patrick Jubb, Australia**
Fewer than 24 hours have elapsed since this baby was born. In a busy hospital ward in Penrith, Australia, the baby is cradled by his mother as he experiences his first bath.

Page 7
© **Karsten Thielker, Germany**
Covering war-torn Bosnia in 1995 became so depressing that the photographer decided to create, alongside the daily horror, a series on newborns. The babies have just been fed and are ready to sleep.

Pages 8–9
© **Andrew Gorrie, New Zealand**
Baby Elena, wrapped tightly in warm blankets, signifies she is awake by punching the air with her fist, as if to say 'Freedom at last!'.

Page 10
© **Karsten Thielker, Germany**
Part of the series on newborns photographed in war-torn Sarajevo (see above). In a local hospital in Sarajevo, a newborn is being weighed for the first time.

Page 11
© **Martin Langer, Germany**
The photographer's dark-haired newborn, Emma, born in Hamburg in January 2001.

Page 13
© **Mark LaRocca, USA**
A mother's joyous smile as she admires her newborn baby, Cedric, born 36 hours ago at this hospital in Newton, Massachusetts, USA.

Pages 14–15 and front cover
© **Christel Dhuit, New Zealand**
They may be twins, but their reactions are very different. Five-month-old sisters in Auckland, New Zealand.

Pages 16–17
© **Stefano Azario, UK**
At a New York airport, there's still time for nine-month-old Verity and her mother Lydzia to play before the long flight home to England.

Page 19
© **Ário Gonçalves, Brazil**
In Alvorado, Brazil, a gentle kiss from her mother, Rosângela, elicits a happy gurgle from three-month-old Ariane.

Page 20
© **Fredé Spencer, Denmark**
Swimming underwater comes perfectly naturally to baby Louis. He and his mother, Dimiti, enjoy a swimming class for "Little Dippers" in London, England.

Page 21
© **Álvaro Diaz, Brazil**
10-month-old Gabriel and his mother, Paula. The photographer captured this picture of his son in Florianopolis, Brazil.

Pages 22–23
© **Stacey P Morgan, USA**
In New York, Anne and her young son Robert discover that the bedroom is the perfect place for hide and seek.

Page 25
© **Milo Stewart Jr, USA**
In Cooperstown, New York, new mother Leslie is enchanted with her baby son Bartow.

Pages 26–27
© **Yew Fatt Siew, Malaysia**
A Buddhist festival at Labuleng Lamasery in Gansu, China – in sub-zero temperatures, a Tibetan mother's embrace offers protection and warmth.

Pages 28–29
© **Emma Bass, New Zealand**
Daughter, Olive Rose, at seven months, exploring her mother's – the photographer's – hand.

Page 30
© **Louise Gubb, South Africa**
The simple love of a family bonds a father and son beside the Fiherenana River in Madagascar. The Malagasy people come to this area to mine for sapphires.

Pages 32–33
© **Shannon Eckstein, Canada**
New father Davy finds the perfect way to bond with his baby daughter, Ciara, only nine days old.

Page 35
© **Gordon Trice, USA**
Father Heath holds his eight-month-old daughter, Bethany. This family portrait was photographed in Abilene, Texas, USA.

Pages 36–37
© Lorenz Kienzle, Germany
A family lies in relaxed contentment on the shore of the River Elbe in Germany. While his parents sleep off their picnic lunch, three-month-old Jan enjoys a drink of his own.

Page 39
© Terry Winn, New Zealand
Jeremy Bakalich, six-months-old at the time, plays 'Boo' whilst waiting to have his studio portrait taken.

Page 40
© Cheryl Shoji, Canada
In Burnaby, British Columbia, Canada, proud grandmother Dorothy soothes her first grandson as he expresses displeasure at a not-so-dry diaper.

Page 42-43
© Henry Hill, USA
Eight-day-old Cyrus is content and secure as he lies sleepily on his father Joe. The young baby had only just left hospital and this image was taken on his first day at home in Colorado Springs, Colorado, USA.

Page 44
© David MacNeill, USA
Just six and a half months old, the photographer's daughter, Madison (Madi), revels in taking a bath.

Page 45
© Marcio RM, Brazil
Thais, at two and a half months, is hungry. She wants to be fed – and doesn't like waiting.

Page 47
© Bill Frantz, USA
Budding saxophonist Sarah, aged two, entertains her baby sister, Leslie, in Wisconsin, USA.

Pages 48–49
© Russell Shakespeare, Australia
In Manly, New South Wales, Australia, five-month-old Camille has a captive audience in her mother, Toni, and visiting grandparents, Margaret and Handley.

Pages 50–51
© Linda Heim, USA
Lynn and her 10-month-old son, Casey, try a new variation of rock-a-bye-baby on the shore of Burden Lake in New York state, USA.

Pages 52–53
© Anne Bayin, Canada
Kim grew up thinking boys would find her unattractive because of her scars, but today she is married and living in Canada. She is a Goodwill Ambassador for UNESCO. This photograph celebrates the first birthday of Kim's son, Thomas.

Kim Phuc was the subject of the most famous picture of the Vietnam War. Taken in 1972,the photograph showed Kim – "the girl in the picture" – badly burned by napalm.

Page 55
© David Williams, UK
In Newcastle, England, godfather David meets his one-month-old godson, Samuel, for the first time.

Pages 56–57
© Quoc Tuan, Vietnam
A grandfather and grandmother, both over the age of 70, are enchanted with their one-month-old grandson. They are playing with him on the verandah of their home in Ho Chi Minh City, Vietnam. The child was born on the couple's 50th wedding anniversary.

Page 58
© Lloyd Erlick, Canada
Proud mother Caitlin gently holds six-month-old Shai as she reaches out to greet her great-grandmother, Natalie.

Page 61
© Kishore Sanghavi, India
The photographer has captured the sheer radiance of young Naju Niraj Mehta, photographed in his house with natural lighting.

Back cover
© Slim Labidi, France
One-month-old Malik is the centre of attention for his loving parents, Cecile and Hafid, photographed at their home in Villeurbaine, France.

Inspired by the 1950s landmark photographic exhibition, *"The Family of Man,"* M.I.L.K. began as an epic global search to develop a collection of extraordinary and geographically diverse images portraying humanity's Moments of Intimacy, Laughter and Kinship (M.I.L.K.). This search took the form of a photographic competition – probably the biggest, and almost certainly the most ambitious of its kind ever to be conducted. With a world-record prize pool, and renowned Magnum photographer Elliott Erwitt as Chief Judge, the M.I.L.K. competition attracted 17,000 photographers from 164 countries. Three hundred winning images were chosen from the over 40,000 photographs submitted to form the basis of the M.I.L.K. Collection.

The winning photographs were first published as three books titled *Family*, *Friendship* and *Love* in early 2001, and are now featured in a range of products worldwide, in nine languages in more than 20 countries. The M.I.L.K. Collection also forms the basis of an international travelling exhibition.

The M.I.L.K. Collection portrays unforgettable images of human life, from its first fragile moments to its last. They tell us that the rich bond that exists between families and friends is universal. Representing many diverse cultures, the compelling and powerful photographs convey feelings experienced by people around the globe. Transcending borders, the M.I.L.K. imagery reaches across continents to celebrate and reveal the heart of humanity.

www.milkphotos.com

First published by Helen Exley Giftbooks in 2005, 16 Chalk Hill, Watford, Herts, WD19 4BG, UK.
www.helenexleygiftbooks.com

12 11 10 9 8 7 6 5 4 3 2 1

ISBN 1-905130-01-5

Designed by Kylie Nicholls. Printed by Midas Printing International Limited, Hong Kong. Back cover quotation by Bob Alberti.

M · I · L · K ™

MOMENTS INTIMACY LAUGHTER KINSHIP